1   Sharpness on the River Severn was developed after
the building of the Gloucester Ship Canal which enabled
relatively big vessels to reach Gloucester (see Plate 2)
and new docks were opened in 1874. This photograph
shows the Swedish wooden barque *Sally*, built at Bath,
Maine, U.S.A., in the local drydock being resheathed
with yellow metal to protect her against the marine boring
pests which were a very great problem with wooden
vessels, even in temperate zones. The photograph shows
the bow ports through which the big lumber the *Sally*
frequently carried to Britain was loaded at Quebec and in
Baltic ports

2   *Frontispiece, overleaf* In 1887 the barque *Mathias*,
built at Vederlax on the Gulf of Finland in 1876 and
under the Russian flag because Finland was then part of
Russia, brought a cargo of Baltic timber to Gloucester
Docks. The timber trade to Gloucester from Canada and
the Baltic developed after the opening of the ship canal to
Gloucester from Sharpness on the Severn in 1827. The
Mathias of Åbo was owned by at least 23 people in the
neighbourhood of Åbo and Kimito, most of whom had
from two to seven one hundredth part shares in her. In
the background can be seen a three-masted schooner
which, from the style of her masts and rigging is also
Finnish or perhaps Swedish

Victorian and Edwardian

Ships and Harbours

from old photographs

BASIL GREENHILL
and
ANN GIFFARD

B.T. Batsford Ltd
London

To Tricia with many thanks

Also by Basil Greenhill and Ann Giffard:
Westcountrymen in Prince Edward's Isle
  (American Association Award: Filmed: Televised)
The Merchant Sailing Ship: A Photographic History
Travelling by Sea in the Nineteenth Century
Women Under Sail
Victorian and Edwardian Sailing Ships

By Basil Greenhill:
The Merchant Schooners (2 volumes)
Sailing for a Living
Out of Appledore (with W.J. Slade)
Boats and Boatmen of Pakistan
Steam and Sail (with Rear Admiral P.W. Brock)
Westcountry Coasting Ketches (with W.J. Slade)
A Victorian Maritime Album
The Coastal Trade (with Lionel Willis)
A Quayside Camera
Archaeology of the Boat

First published 1978
Copyright B. Greenhill and A. Giffard 1978

Filmset in 'Monophoto' Apollo by
Servis Filmsetting Ltd, Manchester
Printed in Great Britain by Cox & Wyman Ltd, Fakenham,
for the publishers B.T. Batsford Ltd,
4 Fitzhardinge St, London W1H 0AH

ISBN 0 7134 1079 5

Contents

Acknowledgments

Introduction

Acknowledgments

National Maritime Museum: 3, 7, 9, 10, 11, 12, 13, 14, 15, 16, 19, 20, 21, 22, 23, 25, 26, 27, 28, 29, 30, 33, 34, 35, 36, 37, 39, 40, 41, 42, 45, 46, 47, 51, 52, 54, 55, 56, 57, 58, 59, 60, 61, 62, 63, 64, 65, 66, 67, 69, 71, 72, 73, 77, 80, 82, 85, 87, 89, 90, 91, 92, 93, 94, 95, 96, 99, 100, 101, 102, 103, 104, 107, 109, 111, 112, 113, 114, 115, 116, 117, 118, 119, 120, 121, 122, 123, 124, 125;

Basil Greenhill and Ann Giffard: 24, 43, 44, 50, 70, 74, 75, 79, 81, 83;
Victorian and Albert Museum: 31, 32, 84;
Captain Wilfred Rowles: 68;
J. Dew: 76;
Gillis Collection: 88;
County Archives of Gwynedd: 97, 98;
Merseyside County Museums: 110.

Introduction

THE PHOTOGRAPHS which follow have been chosen, very largely from the collection in the National Maritime Museum, to illustrate different aspects of the life of ports and harbours around the coasts of Britain in the last century and a half.

This is the second of three books in the 'Victorian and Edwardian' series dealing exclusively with maritime historical photographs. The first was *Victorian and Edwardian Sailing Ships*. The third will be *Victorian and Edwardian Steamships*. The subjects of these two books are clear and almost mutually exclusive. The present collection of photographs comes in between the other two and involves the subjects of both of them, because in photographs of Victorian and Edwardian ports and harbours sailing vessels almost invariably appear, as in the later photographs do more and more steamers. These ships demand attention and are usually the reason for the photograph having been taken, or at least for the subject having been composed in a particular way. The interest of the dock or harbour itself was often incidental to the photograph, unless the photograph was of, say, a busy scene on Merseyside with the ferries coming and going, or of a Scottish or Cornish cove in which the ships and boats are incidental to the scenery. Sometimes, in the absence of photographs of local shipbuilding, this has involved using a photograph of a ship to illustrate the products of a port's industry. So, what with one thing and another, the ships play a large part in the subject matter of the photographs in this book, as they do in the other two. This book, therefore, overlaps the other two in subject matter to a degree to which they do not overlap each other.

In *Victorian and Edwardian Sailing Ships* we described and illustrated the classic types of sailing ships of the era, barques, brigs, schooners and so on. We have used the terms in this book, but have not repeated the definitions here. We have had to use the terms because in the photographs of vessels lying in the harbours sailing ships predominate. This is inevitable, because sailing vessels continued to be more numerous than steamships until well into the later Victorian era. There were good reasons for this. To anticipate *Victorian and Edwardian Steamships* a little, the steamship could not compete economically in general world trade until three products of Victorian engineering and industrial development had been brought together. Iron had to be available cheaply and in shaped pieces of large dimensions. Because for various reasons paddles were not efficient at sea the screw propeller had to be developed to a reasonably high level of efficiency and this itself posed engineering problems. Finally, a really efficient and economical steam engine had to be developed and built in numbers to drive the screws. This engine as it was developed worked at higher steam pressures than its predecessors and this requirement in its turn meant that boilers had to be developed to match the engines – again a complex technical achievement.

The combination of iron construction, screw propulsion and efficient, economical, compound engines, driven by steam from boilers working at relatively high pressure, did not begin to be achieved commercially until the mid-1860s. But even then, two other developments were required before the steamship could really compete with sailing vessels, which after 1870 themselves developed very rapidly until the bigger ones, steel four-masted barques and multi-masted schooners, bore little resemblance to their predecessors.

To load cargo in paying quantities steamships

had to be freed from the necessity of carrying enough coal to take them to the far ends of the earth. This meant that bunkering stations had to be established, as far as Britain was concerned at key points under British control, on the principal trade routes on which British ships were employed. Until yet further developments in making steamships more economical took place the carrying of coal in bulk was a job which sailing vessels could do more cheaply. So the very development of steam gave rise to more work for sailing vessels which continued to be seen lying in British harbours in large numbers.

The second development is immediately relevant to the subject of the photographs in this book. Steamships were very expensive to run in comparison with sailing vessels, and especially expensive to keep lying in harbour loading and discharging cargo – or waiting to load or discharge. Economical, efficient, steamships on the world's major trade routes, using coal from bunkering stations served by sailing vessels, could only operate profitably if the facilities were efficient in the ports they used.

In industrial development at any period, things rarely go smoothly or simply, but as the demand for better facilities developed as a result of the increased effectiveness of steamships in competition for the world carrying trade, so harbours and docks in Britain were improved, at first slowly, and then rapidly, so that the appearance of many harbours changed out of all recognition in late Victorian and Edwardian times. But even in the 1870s the majority of the world's sea carriers were still wooden sailing ships, and it was not until the next decade that steamers really began rapidly to dominate the trade routes and consequently to be in due course the most numerous vessels seen lying in British ports and harbours.

At the same time the changes in the appearance of many harbours where much cargo was loaded and discharged took place. At the beginning of the Victorian era, though there were some enclosed docks where vessels could lie afloat unaffected by the tides, most harbours were still tidal, and the flat-bottomed wooden

sailing ships which comprised by far the majority of vessels using them had to lie on the mud or the sand of the harbour floor at low tides (Plate 93). The endless rise and fall of vessels up and down the quay walls as the tide flowed and ebbed made loading and discharging difficult and slow. Many shipping places could only be used at spring tides, because the channels which gave access to them were too shallow during neaps, and these conditions also imposed limitations on the sizes of the vessels which could be employed in trade to such places.

The Victorian and Edwardian eras saw the deepening of channels, the construction of floating docks, the provision of warehouses, cranes, railway systems, of refrigeration in docks, and, in due course, for bulk cargoes such as coal and other materials, of automatic loading devices of varying degrees of sophistication. They saw also the construction of housing and shops for the great population of casual labourers who worked the cargoes, despite the gradual introduction of mechanical methods. They saw the development of some small harbours out of all recognition into new important dock systems.

But some of the small ports and harbours which survived unchanged kept their identity throughout the era and some were scarcely altered at the end of the period from their appearance and function and significance to the local community at the beginning. It took the development of road transport, after the end of Edwardian times to bring to an end the centuries old activities of small sailing vessels which carried small cargoes to serve local areas. The vessels developed in Victorian times. Smacks, brigs and brigantines with round bows and deep hulls gave way to ketches and schooners of better hull design, capable of making many more voyages than their predecessors with paying cargo each year, and in greater safety. But some of the little cracks in the rocks and the beaches and the small tidal docks to which they sailed all round the coasts of Britain changed little during the period covered by this book (Plates 63 and 81).

It is necessary perhaps at this stage to define

the terms 'port' and 'harbour'. Properly speaking the term port denotes, not a particular harbour town, but an officially delimited length of coast line, including any embraced 'member ports' or 'creeks'. Thus Chester once embraced Liverpool and Caernarvon and in the great days of its Victorian prosperity Porthmadog was a creek of the now independent Port of Caernarvon and its vessels bore the name of Caernarvon on their sterns. A port thus might comprise several harbours, portions of the sea naturally or artificially protected, so as to be places of safety, for vessels to lie while loading, discharging, waiting or sheltering, and it might also include shipping places, such as beaches, not perhaps natural harbours, where vessels loaded or discharged or laid up from time to time, or loading and discharging places or tidal creeks far inland, remote backwaters of great harbours, like the quays on the Tamar or the Truro or Tresillian rivers in Cornwall.

We have attempted to illustrate the development of ports and harbours with varying degrees of completeness, not in any sense in sequence, but in the selection of photographs which show in one place or another some of the aspects of change in ports in the late nineteenth and early twentieth centuries. At the same time, like all other forms of industrial activity, in the last resort the developments were the results of human activity. So human beings can be seen in many of the pictures, sometimes as small details, tiny figures tidying up the fo'c'sle after a vessel has been anchored, or shouting across the gap between two ships waiting to load cargo, sometimes in the forefront. Among them are a few members of the great army of dock labourers of one kind or another who made it possible for trade to be carried on with what seems to us now pitifully few mechanical aids to human toil.

3 Many people see the acme of the trans-Atlantic passenger trade by sea as achieved not by the *Queen Elizabeth II* or even the *Queen Mary* but by the first *Mauretania*, here seen watched by a great crowd as she leaves the Tyne, where she was built, for the first time after her completion in 1907. She was the first big turbine-engined vessel, and had a brilliantly successful career, holding the 'Blue Riband', the Atlantic speed record, and providing with the *Berengaria* and the *Aquitania* 'the fastest Ocean service in the world'. This photograph epitomises the industrial vigour of the river Tyne before the First World War

4 *Right* Blyth Harbour was one of the historic coal ports of the North East. The home of a great fleet of collier brigs in mid-Victorian times – 200 vessels were owned there in 1874, the harbour was deepened and facilities improved to take steam colliers in the later part of the century. This photograph shows the Danish steamer *Hamlet* entering to load. Notice the hobbler towed behind in his coble – the local type of working boat. He will help to secure the *Hamlet* in her berth. The life of Blyth in Victorian times was brilliantly described by the first Lord Runciman in his splendid book *Collier Brigs and Their Sailors*, recently made available in a modern reprint

The North-east Coast

ALTHOUGH all the big ports altered out of all recognition in Victorian times perhaps the most dramatic development took place on the north-east coast. Here the expansion of the coal-carrying business was only too visible. And this was an increase of business above a very high level already existing in early Victorian times – for instance, in 1856 already five million tons of coal were carried in coastal sailing vessels from the Tyne, Wear and Tees, mainly to London. These were ports where the potentialities of the iron screw steamer were recognised and exploited at an early date. By the '80s the old locally-owned square-rigged sailing vessels of the coal trade to London which had existed in the 1850s and '60s in such vast numbers were already nearly all gone. The first Lord Runciman summed up late Victorian and Edwardian progress on the north-east coast very well when he wrote in his splendid book *Collier Brigs and Their Sailors* of Blyth, 'The barque I commanded . . . carried about 750 tons and was much too large for the port until long after I had left her. . . . In 1885 the first steamer I owned had to wait outside the harbour until half-tide before she could enter in ballast, and her light draught was only nine to ten feet. Twelve thousand tonners pass in and out with ease now.

'The whole bed of the rocky bottom has been blasted out, and no better facilities for loading coal exist anywhere.'

5 *Above* Inside the harbour at Blyth the early iron steam
colliers *Weardale* and *Rouen*, the latter built at
Newcastle-on-Tyne in 1857 and one of the first steamers
to be fitted with water ballast tanks, both heavily rigged
as schooners, lie at the tips or 'staithes' which, by
speeding up the process of loading, greatly improved the
port's efficiency in mid-Victorian times

6 *Above* The *Victoria* leaves her building place on the Tyne on 6 April 1888, passing from Elswick under the High Level Bridge and through the Swing Bridge on her way to sea. Her armament has not yet been fitted. This was the ship lost by collision with the *Camperdown* on 22 June 1893, in circumstances never fully explained. Note the steam barge on the right

7 *Left* This photograph of the old Redheugh Bridge over the River Tyne, which was replaced in Edwardian times, is of especial interest because it shows an old clinker-built wooden paddle tug towing three of the famous Tyne keels. These were sailing barges, used to take the coal from the riverside coal shutes to the anchored colliers for centuries before the river was deepened and the tips downstream of the bridges developed so that vessels could load alongside. These keels were smooth-skinned vessels, the planks of which were not joined together at the edges. They were replaced in Victorian times by larger barges, clinker-built, locally called wherries. Two of these can be seen towed immediately astern of the tug

8   *Above* Tyne Dock, opened in 1859, was one of the
first examples of a dock laid out to facilitate the loading
of steamers, using as did most north-east coast ports, the
high banks of the river to bring the railway wagons
above the ships. The barques *Lalla Rookh* (left) and
Largiemore however appear to be unloading timber. The
former was a long-lived vessel built at Hull in 1876 which
finished her career in the 1930s under the ownership of
Gustaf Erikson of the Åland Islands, the world's last
owner of large deep-sea square-rigged sailing ships. The
Largiemore, built on the Clyde in 1892, went missing
while under the Norwegian flag in 1914

9   *Above right* The steamer *Rowan* lies loading under a
coal tip at West Hartlepool while at least eight square-
rigged sailing vessels await their turns at the loading
berths to take on board coal cargoes for delivery all over
the world. It was the custom in many coal ports before
the First World War to give steamers, which had much
higher expenses in port than sailing vessels, preference in
turn for loading. When delays were excessive this could
cause much bad feeling and regular traders with a good
sailing record, like the famous barquentine *Waterwitch*
which carried coal from Seaham Harbour to Portsmouth
for many years and became Britain's last square-rigged
merchant sailing ship at sea, were given a steamer's turn
round

10   *Right* A view of the great Elswick works on the
Tyne in their heyday. Founded by Sir William
Armstrong in the 1850s, the works expanded so that they
could design and build warships and their guns from raw
material to completion. Two warships can be seen
completing in the distance. In the foreground, colliers
wait for their turn at the staithes up-river of Newcastle

50023. Bridlington Harbour. F.F.& Co.

11 *Above left* Whitby is one of Britain's historic ports, associated with the coal trade in which many of its vessels were employed, with world trade generally, and with shipbuilding. Lacking industrial hinterland, like Bideford in Devon its industry in Victorian times was the ocean carrying trade. The paddle steamer loaded with passengers is the *Scarborough* and the boats are local cobles and mules

12 *Above* In the period covered by this book Bridlington was a coasting harbour with local fishing and what is now called the tourist trade. This photograph shows the handsome paddle tug *Frenchman* of Hull entering the harbour in the course of her profitable summer employment of running passengers on excursions. Notice how in those regulation-free days even the bridge was crowded with visitors

13 This great fishing fleet was photographed off Scarborough, but seems to comprise almost entirely Lowestoft boats. Taken in the 1880s the photograph shows the Lowestoft fishing fleet in the transition period when trawling was developing and the lug sails long used by the drifters with their long curtains of net were giving way to the ketch rig, which was more suitable for the new fishing method. The ketch rig developed more power to pull the beam trawls, and the fish they caught could be readily marketed because of the development of the railway system and the increasing population

14 *Left* One of the commonest sights in Victorian and Edwardian times, particularly in the ports of the north east of England, was the Scandinavian or Russian/Finnish wooden barque or brig laden with a cargo of Norwegian or Baltic timber. Here is the brig *Hilding* warping – that is, being pulled with her own ropes – into dock at Hull in May, 1906

15 *Below* The Alexandra Dock at Hull at the beginning of the present century. The steamer in the foreground is discharging through shutes into barges. A Humber keel, the local type of sailing barge, lies under the exhaust jet from one of her steam winches aft. The big steamer in the background is the *Dido* built at Hull in 1896

47170. Selby; The River. F.F&Cº.

16 *Above* Taken, probably on a Sunday, in 1901, this photograph shows the yard of the Selby Shipbuilding and Engineering Co Ltd with two new vessels, a steam trawler and a steam coaster, alongside and another under construction on the slipway. Selby, far inland as it was, was a shipbuilding centre of some importance on the network of navigable waterways which brought seagoing vessels far into the heart of Yorkshire

The East Coast

THE SHADOW of the great coal trade reached over many ports and harbours on the east coast of England. Some which did not export coal themselves, like Whitby, were nevertheless deeply involved in the trade. Whitby is a good example of a Victorian and pre-Victorian phenomenon, a port without great industrial hinterland which made its industry the carrying trade – the provision of the means to move other people's cargoes between distant ports. Whitby also had an active shipbuilding industry.

Hull was the home of a whaling fleet and later on a great fishing industry as well as of an extensive world and continental trade. Grimsby was the greatest fishing port in the world at one stage of the period covered by this book. Lowestoft and Yarmouth were likewise known as the homes of great fishing fleets.

17 *Left* The first dock at Grimsby was opened at the beginning of the last century, but the development of Grimsby was a product of Victorian times when, as a result of the enterprise of the Manchester, Sheffield and Lincolnshire Railway Company, Grimsby became the greatest fishing port in the country. This photograph shows the commercial side of the port. Among the seven steamers and ten sailing vessels visible are the barque *Warden Law*, the barquentine *Violet*, built at New Bideford, Prince Edward Island, Canada, and the schooner *Pride of Anglesey* from Beaumaris

18 *Above* This photograph, taken in the 1880s, shows the other side of Grimsby's work, a dock filled with sailing trawlers. In the 1850s there was one fishing vessel sailing out of Grimsby, in 1891 there were 800 sailing and 35 steam trawlers. Ten years later the position was reversed, with nearly 500 steam trawlers and only 34 large sailing vessels. In the foreground in this photograph are Sheringham fishermen who migrated along the coast in the late nineteenth century, taking their characteristic double-ended boats with them by train

19 Three early steam trawlers in dock at Boston in
Lincolnshire. They are beam trawlers, like the sailing
vessels shown in Plate 18, and the photograph must have
been taken between the introduction of screw steamers
into trawling in the 1880s and the general adoption of the
otter trawl by steam trawlers in the late 1890s

20 This photograph was taken on 23 August 1890 and it shows the harbour at Lowestoft, also a great fishing port, with two trawlers on their way out to the fishing grounds under sail without the use of a tug. As with Grimsby, Lowestoft's history as a fishing port is a product of the nineteenth century. In 1863 there were eight trawlers. At the end of Queen Victoria's reign the port had 233 drifters and 247 trawlers, all sailing vessels

21 Like Grimsby, Lowestoft had an extensive cargo business as well as a great fishery. This photograph shows the commercial side of the port's work, with the Norwegian brigantine *Vidfarne*, of Brevig, in the foreground and a very typical small wooden barque on the other side of the harbour. Ahead of her men are discharging the cargo of an equally typical Norfolk wherry, the sailing barge of the Norfolk Broads, her black sail flapping idly on what is evidently a calm summer's day

22 A member of the crew was standing on the fo'c'sle head of the brig *Evelyn* of Porthmadog when she was photographed in Yarmouth Harbour. The *Evelyn* was the last brig-rigged merchant sailing vessel working out of a home port in the United Kingdom. Yarmouth, like Lowestoft and Grimsby, was known all over the world as a fishing port, but it also had an extensive trade, especially with continental ports

23 St Osyth, near Clacton, was a creek involved with
one of the important trades of the London River sailing
barges, the bringing to the capital of vast quantities of
hay needed to feed the thousands of horses which worked
in the streets. The cargo of this barge has come down to
the waterside in farm carts and, now she is loaded, she is
waiting to leave on the flood tide. The floating haystack
is so high that she can set only half her huge mainsail.
She will return with another valuable cargo – horse
manure for the local farms from the city streets and
stables

24 *Below* The Norwegian brig *S N Hansen* entering an east coast harbour. Sail is being taken in as a local boat alongside puts men on board. They will help to make her fast when she reaches her berth. Hobblers, or hovellers, as such men were usually known, were a feature of Victorian and Edwardian ports and they are shown at work in several photographs in this book

25 Ramsgate, despite its proximity to the London market, started late as the home port of a large fishing fleet. In the early nineteenth century Brixham vessels used its harbour extensively but by the 1880s and 90s Ramsgate had a fine fishing fleet of its own comprised of vessels built in many different places on the south and east coasts of Britain. There was also a prosperous commercial trade, partly in timber with the Baltic. This photograph shows ten local sailing trawlers and three merchant sailing ships in the harbour

26 *Above right* Another aspect of the life of Ramsgate, yachts in the foreground and units of the fishing fleet and a solitary merchant vessel in the background. Passengers crowd into wagonettes and the front is teeming with visitors brought by the railway or steamers from London and most of them, no doubt, staying in the local boarding houses and lodgings

27 *Right* In Victorian and Edwardian times the Downs, the stretch of water off Deal in Kent, provided a kind of natural harbour and a good anchorage for sailing vessels awaiting a fair wind down the English Channel. Many vessels sailed out of London or down the North Sea in the prevailing westerlies or south-westerlies. Beyond Deal these winds were useless for square-rigged vessels in tidal waters and they collected in the Downs by the hundred to await a favourable easterly or northerly wind. The photograph taken in the 1870s shows only 68 square-rigged vessels of various kinds at anchor

28 Eight brothers and their mother proudly stand on the hatch and side deck of the new London River sailing barge *Eight Brothers* built at Chiswick in 1894. The new suit of sails and the splendid name pendant were made by Gill & Sons, sailmakers of Rochester. Sailing barges like this one loaded and discharged at many wharves and hards above bridges as far as the head of tidewater, all of which were technically part of the port of London

29 *Right* This cluster of shipping at Wapping, a schooner, a brig, a brigantine, wooden lighters, dates from the 1850s or 60s. By the loading shute on the left-hand side of the picture is just visible a group of men in stove pipe tall hats, similar in shape to the funnel of the little steamer in the foreground

London River

LONDON for the greater part of the period covered by this book was the greatest port in Britain and one of the greatest in the world. The port comprised the whole of London river – from tidewater head to the limits from Havengore Creek to Warden Port on either side of the estuary. The centre of the port's trade was, of course, in the docks, built largely in the eighteenth and nineteenth centuries and culminating in the construction of King George V Dock in the post-Edwardian era. But numerous wharves all the way up and down the river were part of the Port of London too. They were served by small vessels and in particular by the ubiquitous London River sailing barges, with their huge red/brown spritsails, which sailed the river in their thousands and were a vital part of its life.

London was also a centre of the shipping industry. Here were the exchanges where vessels were 'fixed' with cargoes, and the centre of the marine insurance world with its survey and classification organisations, the centre for shipping finance and of the commodity markets. The London River also had an extensive shipbuilding industry.

30 The South West India Dock was built between 1866 and 1870 and was used by vessels in the Colonial and Indian trades. The lighters in the foreground are filled with heavy engineering equipment which appears to be being loaded into the full-rigged ship immediately behind the steamer's funnel

31 *Above right* This is also the South West India Dock, photographed from the quayside. The vessel nearest the camera on the right-hand side is discharging a part cargo of hemp in loose bales. Note the London River barges with their spritsails

32 Fosters Wharf, Lower Pool, London, at about the end of the era covered by this book. A cargo in bags is being discharged into a lighter. A steam collier, three London River sailing barges of different kinds, and a Dutch ketch fill the foreground

33 *Right* This was the riverside at Lambeth, looking towards Vauxhall, with the houses backing on to the water, before the Embankment was built

34 *Below* In this photograph the building of the embankment, which began the process of controlling the flooding tide of the Thames, has started at Lambeth. London River sailing barges lie on the foreshore. The one behind the oarsman in the river skiff is of a very old type

35 *Below* Hundreds of auxiliary sailing vessels were built in Holland and Scandinavia during the transition from sail to diesel power in the first quarter of this century. But although many old sailing vessels were adapted to be motorships, only two or three vessels were built as auxiliary motorships in Britain. This one, the *Motoketch*, just launched at Millwall at the end of the Edwardian era, was one of the last two merchant sailing vessels, other than London River barges, to be built on the Thames. She had a long and successful career.

36 *Right* Part of the crew are gathered on the forecastle-head of the splendid steel four-masted barque *Arthur Sewall*, just moored to a buoy off Gravesend on 3 April 1900, with the tugs still alongside. She was one of the very few big steel sailing vessels to be built in the United States. She is waiting to go up to her berth in one of the docks

37 A hay barge, see Plate 23, at the other end of her passage to a City wharf from an Essex creek. As she comes slowly up to her berth in the Pool of London the mate cons from the top of the cargo – the master at the tiller is entirely dependent on him for steering the barge. The paddle steamer in the background is the *Swallow*

38 This old London River sailing barge is about to pass under London Bridge on the flood tide. Her crew are lowering her 'bridge sail', a standing lug set from a short mast set up in place of the lowered mainmast when working above bridges. She is evidently going far up river

39 A barque discharging small timber from the Baltic in the Regent's Canal Dock. The cargo is being loaded into lighters

THE THAMES BELOW LONDON BRIDGE 2005 GWW

40 *Above* This photograph was taken just below London Bridge in the early 1870s. It is full of activity: Dutch eel boats, a London steam trawler, steam coasters, a small full-rigged ship, lighters, skiffs, and people crowding the steps on the right-hand side of the photograph

41 Folkstone, the other great packet port of the narrow
seas, as photographed by Francis Frith in the early 1890s.
Men on a staging are caulking new planks on the
brigantine in the centre of the picture. It is a hot
summer's day and a water cart has recently passed by to
lay the dust on the dirt road. It has left clear evidence of
its turn in the immediate foreground.

42 *Right* Dover in the late 1860s. The bell top funnelled
paddle steam packet in the centre is the *Etoile du Nord*
built in 1862 and the brig on the left, with her single
topsails stowed in the bunt in the manner of HMS
Victory is the *Cyprian Queen* built in 1860. Note the swan-
neck crane to the right of the steam packet

The South Coast

THE LONG south coast has historic ports, like Rye and Winchelsea, Fowey and Dartmouth. It has magnificent natural harbours, like Falmouth and Plymouth. It has in Southampton one of the major ports of Britain and it has the two great naval bases at Devonport and Portsmouth. It has the channel ferry terminals and besides all these it has many small harbours, creeks and beaches where trade and fishing have been carried on for centuries.

During the period covered by this book Fowey developed as a great port of export of china clay and on a smaller scale as a port involved with the historic trade in dried fish with Newfoundland. Falmouth became a national as well as a regional port, so that in 1872 about 7,500 vessels used the harbour in one way or another. Devonport developed to accommodate the new steam navy, as did also Portsmouth. The packet ports of New Haven, Dover and Folkestone grew out of recognition as did also Southampton, so dramatically that by the end of the period it challenged Liverpool as the principal port of the Atlantic passenger trade.

43 The supreme skill and confidence with which
Victorian and Edwardian merchant seamen handled their
vessels under sail is well illustrated by this photograph of
the schooner *Elizabeth Bennet*, built at Runcorn in 1884,
entering a Channel port. She is almost between the piers,
yet only now are four of her crew, leaving the fifth,
probably the master, at the wheel, busy at the foot of the
mainmast taking in the main gaff topsail, and she is still
sailing hard, close hauled on the starboard tack

44 This photograph, taken at Littlehampton, illustrates 50 years of development in sailing ship design. The old brig *Mitchelgrove* of Arundel, built at Arundel in 1815, full-lined, with tumble home, heavy stern and high bulwarks, compares with the sweet lined clipper brig or snow, *Emma*, newly launched from Harvey's Yard on the bright day in 1866 when this photograph was taken. Harvey's of Littlehampton were prominent shipbuilders in the later nineteenth and early twentieth centuries

LITTLEHAMPTON.

45 *Left* This photograph shows Littlehampton when it was a thriving port and shipbuilding centre. The ketch in the foreground is the *Charlotte Sophia* of Portsmouth; astern of her is what looks like a Swedish or Finnish Russian *skonnertskepp*, no doubt discharging a timber cargo, then a steel-hulled ketch from Holland, then two vessels discharging coal, the steam coaster *Onyx* of Ipswich built at Dumbarton in 1883 and the shallow draft schooner *Zebrina* of Faversham. The *Zebrina* was later to become famous as the vessel found drifting and abandoned off the French coast but in perfect order. The mystery of what happened to her crew has never been solved

46 *Below* This delightful picture of Littlehampton shows boys in grave danger of trouble for wet feet as they play on timber discharged into a pound by vessels from the Baltic. The vessels illustrated include the barquentine *Sarah Amy* built at Emsworth, a London River ketch-barge and a Swedish *slättoppare*, a three-masted schooner with the masts all the same height and no square yards

47 At the time of Queen Victoria's Diamond Jubilee in 1897 a major naval review was held at Spithead. This photograph was taken looking west and shows part of the vast fleet with numerous yachts and other vessels. To our minds the most handsome vessel there is the 'brig-rigged screw', as she would have been called at the time, the American vessel in the right-hand middle distance

48 *Right* Portsmouth Harbour in the days of wood and sail. The great ship in the foreground is HMS *St Vincent*, a first-rate of 120 guns, built at Devonport between 1810 and 1815. She was still in commission in the mid-1850s when she sailed during the Crimean War as a unit in the great Baltic fleet that was involved with the seige and bombardment of Bomarsund, the Russian fortress in the Åland Islands in the Gulf of Bothnia. The *St Vincent* was not broken up until 1906

60441.

49 This interesting photograph was taken in the summer of 1908 and shows the Empress Dock at Southampton. The tug *Ajax* on the left of the picture belonged to the local Red Funnel Line which still operates passenger and car ferries across to Cowes. Astern of her is the Royal Mail liner *Amazon*, employed in the South American passenger service to the River Plate. She is taking in bunkers from the coal elevator alongside her and the small vessel which is steaming across the dock is bringing additional bunkers for her.

The other vessels are the Union Castle Line's steamers *Norman* and *Saxon,* both berthed to the left of the dock entrance. They carried on the service to South Africa which was terminated only in 1977. The American liner *St Paul* is on the right-hand side of the picture. She was the first passenger liner to be fitted with wireless telegraphy

50 A big crowd waits on Ryde pierhead in the Isle of
Wight to board the paddle steamer *Lorna Doone*, built in
1891, bound towards Bournemouth. This is the Edwardian
era, shortly before the First World War. Piers served as
points of embarkation and disembarkation for passengers,
and for landing and discharging cargo, as well as for
promenades for pleasure

51 At the other end of the journey the steamer *Brodick Castle*, built in 1878, is seen landing passengers on the pier at Bournemouth. At the time the photograph was taken she was running between Bournemouth and Swanage. A pier was especially useful when there was no harbour and the sea was shallow a long way off shore

52 The big three-masted schooner nearest the camera in this photograph of Poole harbour in Dorset is the *Mary Watkinson* of Barrow, owned by James Fisher & Co of that port, who had the biggest fleet of merchant schooners operating out of a home port in Britain in late Victorian times. The vessels are lying two deep all the way down the quay and some of them are completing loading the cargoes of china clay, for which most of them have come to Poole, from barges brought alongside

53 This photograph shows a natural harbour in use in the 1890s. It is Lulworth Cove and the steamer landing passengers over a gangplank straight on to the busy working fishing beach is the *Victoria*

34.570. F.F & C?

54 Bridport in Victorian times was an important centre
of ropemaking and a busy little commercial harbour with
a well-known and successful shipyard where many
vessels were built for owners in Newfoundland. This
photograph shows a Swedish or Russian Finnish
skonnertskepp discharging lumber from the Baltic, several
yachts, and the bows of a British schooner.

55 St Peter Port, Guernsey, with the London and South Western Railway Company's packet steamer *Hilda* about to discharge her cargo from the fore hold into carts, while the passengers embark into the after part of the vessel. *Hilda* was built in 1882

T. S. S. *Hilda*, ... T. Singleton, Phot

56 Many fishing boats did not operate from a harbour at all but from open beaches up which they were pulled after every trip. This is Beer in South Devon with some of its fleet. Even at this time – 1890 – there are some tourists to be seen on the cliff paths

42486. Beer Beach. F.F & Co.

57 Calstock, miles up the tidal river Tamar from the
open sea, was an important shipping place in Victorian
times, because of the extensive mining, quarrying, brick
manufacture, market gardening and farming which were
carried on on the river banks. The steamer loading
granite is the *Albion*, and her cargo is probably destined
to be used in improvements to Dover Harbour

River Tamar, Calstoc

The Jerry, Saltash.   24.

58 The steam chain ferry over the Tamar at Saltash
with the Tamar sailing barge *Flora May*, a vessel engaged
exclusively in carrying cargoes inside the huge area of
Plymouth harbour and the adjacent creeks and rivers.
Many of these cargoes were loaded at wharves belonging
to the local mines, brickworks, quarries and farms and
taken to Plymouth, some for trans-shipment into larger
vessels. Many of the cargoes of grain, manure and
roadstone, were simply carried from one small quay to
another inside the port. These sailing barges performed
the same functions as horse-drawn wagons, but more
quickly and cheaply

59 *Below* Sutton Harbour is the old harbour area of Plymouth, the historic part of the town from which the defenders against the Armada, the Pilgrim Fathers, Captain James Cook and countless others, sailed. This early photograph was taken in 1864 and shows the new brigantine *Lily Annie*, just delivered for local owners from Prince Edward Island in Canada where she was built. The *Lily Annie* has technical details in her rigging which, until this photograph was discovered recently, were not known to have been used in Victorian merchant ships

60 *Above* No one in the world will ever see again a
sight like this, recorded by a photographer who one day
in the 1850s found some 300 sailing vessels lying together
in Plymouth Sound awaiting favourable winds or better
weather

61 The fish market at Sutton Harbour with visiting
steam trawlers from Milford Haven and local sailing
fishing vessels, photographed in mid-Edwardian times

62 *Left* This photograph of the waterfront at Fowey shows the *Little Secret*, one of a fleet of schooners owned by John Stephens of Fowey, which traded between Britain, the Mediterranean and Newfoundland, bringing back Newfoundland salted cod fish, a hard trade which lasted from the sixteenth century until the 1930s. Fowey in Cornwall was a great port in the fourteenth and fifteenth centuries which lapsed in importance thereafter until later Victorian times. New facilities were then built and the port became important for the export of china clay, as it still is. Fowey was almost the last port in Britain to send out small sailing vessels in deep sea trade

63 *Below* Much trade in Victorian times was local, vessels loaded and discharged on open beaches, in coves and cracks in the rock, in creeks often without any harbour facilities at all. The photograph shows this kind of trade. The little schooner is discharging coal on to a creekside wharf with her own gear and a couple of wheel barrows. It will be picked up in carts for the local farms. The scene is believed to be a creek off the estuary of the river Fowey in South Cornwall, but the vessel's name is not known

64 The cart ferry across Fowey Harbour in Cornwall at Bodinnick in the days when it was pulled with sweeps, though it was probably guided with a pair of submerged wire ropes. The vessels in the creek opposite the camera are under repair

65 A busy scene in a south coast fishing port, probably Mevagissey. Notice the traveller from which the yard of the big dipping lug sail of the fishing boat in the foreground was slung and the dipping lug sail set to dry on another boat in the background. In 1850 Mevagissey had 80 fishing vessels employing 300 men, and supporting both their families and ten fish curing businesses

66   *Above* This photograph is full of interesting detail.
Taken on board a sailing trawler in an unknown south
coast harbour, but probably in Cornwall, it shows next to
the companionway William Henry Harris and on the left
the man who became Skipper Pillar and in 1914 put his
trawler alongside the torpedoed HMS *Formidable* and
rescued part of her crew. Here he and William Harris are
shown securing the foot rope of the beam trawl – a
typical harbour maintenance job on board a big fishing
ketch. Note the steam capstan boiler inside the
companionway with its pressure gauge. The success of
beam trawling depended very much on the steam
capstans which greatly reduced the time spent in hauling
the trawl

67 The Plymouth built ketch *Diligent*, discharging salt
at Mevagissey in Edwardian times for a local fish curing
factory which prepared pilchards for export in the
barrels which can be seen on the quay. The *Diligent* is
very similar in type and appearance to the *Shamrock*,
recently restored by the National Maritime Museum and
the National Trust at Cotehele Quay on the Tamar north
of Plymouth

68 To get a boat out of Porthleven in south Cornwall involved towing or 'tracking' her out of the artificial harbour. This was done by four or five men on a tow rope who worked her out while the boat's sails were being set. Porthleven Harbour was built in the early nineteenth century, ostensibly as a harbour of refuge, and much improved in the 1850s. Although there was some trade in china clay and other commodities the harbour never succeeded commercially, though it had, and still has, a fishing fleet, and small wooden merchant sailing vessels, fishing vessels and pilot cutters, were built there

The Bristol Channel
– the English Shore

IN CONTRAST with the opposite coast of Wales, the English shore of the Bristol Channel had only one major port – Bristol, one of the ancient and historic ports of Britain, which, for reasons connected with its inaccessibility up the winding tidal river Avon, gradually lost importance through the Victorian era and only began to recover with the building of the beginnings of Avonmouth Docks towards the end of the century.

But in Victorian times a number of lesser harbours thrived and prospered – Gloucester with its North American and Baltic timber trades, the ship canal and the Sharpness Docks, Bridgwater with its Victorian docks, Bideford with its worldwide carrying trade, its intimate connections with Canada, and its relatively large shipbuilding industry, and Padstow which had a regular trade with North America in Victorian times.

Besides these there were numerous muddy creeks, holes in beaches and cracks in the rock, where coal from the Forest of Dean was discharged from smacks, schooners and ketches for domestic and local industrial use and the products of local mines, quarries and farms were loaded for delivery at the bigger ports.

69 *Left* The barque *Mary Ann Peters* was built at Richibucto in New Brunswick, Canada in 1835. Owned in Bristol, she left the City Docks on 31 March 1857 bound for West Africa and promptly grounded on the old Rownham ferry slip. She was just one of many vessels caught in the Bristol Avon on a falling tide in sailing ship days – and indeed for years into the age of the steamer – and the local riggers, used to the situation, soon had her upper masts and spars down to avoid a capsize as she grounded in the soft mud, listing heavily. She was refloated and sailed another six years until she was lost on the coast of Bermuda in 1863

70 *Above* Bristol, one of the great ports in British history, although less important than in former years still conducted a great overseas trade in Victorian times. Traffic poured up the Avon to Bristol City Docks on the latter part of every flood tide, down on the first of every ebb. This photograph shows the Norwegian barque *Victoria*, built, almost entirely of spruce wood, at the New Bideford Yard, Prince Edward Island, Canada, in 1874, on the same slipways as the barquentine *Violet* (see Plate 17). She has a cargo of timber. Note the hobblers in their boats on the starboard quarter of the *Victoria*. They will help to get her through the locks. Notice also the windmill pump, by which old wooden ships from Scandinavia and Finland were kept afloat without killing their crews from continuous pumping. One of these windmill pumps is now preserved on board the restored wooden barque *Sygin* at Åbo in Finland

71 And this is a place to and from which the vessels in the last two photographs were bound, the old Bristol City Docks as they were in Victorian times, now little used and, in fact, covered over with road development from about where the stern of the steamer is in this photograph. Bristol, with the development of the Avonmouth and West Dock systems, has in recent years regained much of the position it lost to Liverpool in the nineteenth century. The paddle steamer is believed to be *Spicy* which ran a passenger service to Bideford, the barque is the *Louisa* built at Bristol in 1853 and operated in the West Indies sugar and rum trade by the local firm of Thomas Daniel & Co of Berkeley Square

72 The last sailing ship to be built in Bristol was the barque *Favell*, launched in 1895 from the Albion Dockyard, unusually bow first, by Miss Favell Hill, later Lady Miles. The *Favell* spent 40 years under the Russian and Finnish flags and was not broken up until 1937. Today the wonderful steamship *Great Britain* occupies the drydock of which the entrance can be seen on the left-hand side of this picture

73 *Right* Early in Edwardian times the American four-masted schooner *Joseph B Thomas* of Thomaston, Maine, took a cargo of sawn timber to Bristol City Docks. A number of photographs were taken of her, including this splendid one of her discharging opposite the Hotwell's Road, very near the dock where the historic steamship *Great Britain* now lies open to the public. Through a glass it can be seen that one of the three figures leaning over the rail on the starboard quarter is a woman. The wives of some of the masters of these big American schooners lived on board the vessels with their husbands for months on end

74 *Right* Pill, on a creek off the winding Bristol Avon, was the home of many of the then famous Bristol Channel pilots who, in their cutters like this one lying in the mouth of the Pill at anchor, went seeking the incoming ships bound for the Bristol Channel ports far out into the mouth of the Channel and the Atlantic. Note the typical late nineteenth-century steam coaster coming down with the ebb from the City Docks upstream. She is very like the *Robin* now preserved by the Maritime Trust

River Avon from Pill.

75 *Left* The eclipse of the City Docks at Bristol was the consequence of the severe limitation on the size of vessels which could reach them, of limitations on use imposed by the tides and the attendant dangers of the narrow, winding river, so well illustrated in Plate 69. The solution was the building of Avonmouth, now a vast complex of docks on both sides of the River Avon; but when this Victorian photograph with its heavily rigged steamships was taken it comprised only one dock, cut in 1877 out of the marshes on the banks of the River Severn

2. Weston-S-M-Pier, above Kewstoke Road.

76 *Left* One of the authors of this book grew up in a house on the north Somerset coast overlooking the Bristol Channel to the west of the mouth of the Bristol Avon. This coast has a number of tidal creeks wandering into the countryside which were used for trade throughout the period covered by this book and for centuries before. Each of these little 'ports' served a hinterland of farms and villages, latterly mostly with coal from Lydney in Gloucester and from South Wales. This photograph shows the ketch *Wave* of Bridgwater, owned in Clevedon, discharging coal at Lympsham on the river Axe in Edwardian times. One of us remembers seeing the locally well-known ketch *Democrat* discharging here in 1945. She was the last vessel to use the quay

77 *Above* Weston-super-Mare was a product of the Victorian railway age, a resort, not a harbour, but there was some small local trade, and in some conditions vessels could shelter, or anchor to await the tide – so important to work in the Bristol Channel – inside one of the local piers. This vessel shows some of the sailing barges of the Bristol Channel, the Severn trows, at anchor awaiting the flood to take them up to Lydney in Gloucestershire or across to South Wales to load coal for Bridgwater. They probably left Bridgwater early on the ebb tide. Because there is little wind and the tide will flow soon the huge gaff sails have not been lowered

78 In Victorian times the port of Bridgewater had an extensive trade with North America, India and the Baltic. Large square-rigged sailing ships were owned in the town, but it was a great fleet of sailing and steam coasters that gave the port most of its business. A dock was opened in 1841, but the riverside quays in the heart of the town remained the main place of discharge and loading for the numerous local coasters. This Victorian photograph shows no less than nine sailing vessels and the masts of another in the local drydock

79 *Above right* Bridgwater had its own shipyards and a launch was a great occasion. In 1908 the last vessel, the ketch *Irene*, was completed and launched into a river crowded with local steamers and sailing vessels and with its banks packed with spectators. The *Irene* is still afloat employed as a yacht

80 *Right* The harbour of Porlock Weir on the north coast of Somerset is really a lagoon formed by the seas piling up pebbles into an outer ridge. A dock capable of taking vessels up to 14 feet in draught was built in the early nineteenth century and formed a good example of the small harbours which served a limited local area until the end of the Edwardian era and the development of road transport. Several very small smack-rigged merchant vessels, some of them ex-pilot cutters, were owned here. One of them, painted black, is in the immediate foreground. The last cargo to come into Porlock Weir was again in the ketch *Democrat*, of Barnstaple, in about 1950

81 This is one of our favourite photographs: one stormy, rainy, day in Edwardian times three vessels, the *Mary*, a little coasting smack, the locally owned ketch *Lily* built at Penryn in 1899, and, nearest the camera, the ketch *Three Sisters*, built at Plymouth before the Battle of Trafalgar and owned in Bideford, were all discharging their coal cargoes into carts at low tide on the beach at Lynmouth in north Devon. Much of the local trade of Britain until the First World War was carried on in conditions like these, with the aid of little that we nowadays associate with the terms 'port' or 'harbour'

82 *Left* Appledore in North Devon was one of the main small sailing ship places in Britain throughout Victorian and Edwardian times. It was essentially a shipowning place. Without an industrial hinterland its industries were shipbuilding and the world carrying trade. Local vessels traded to North America, to the Mediterranean, to South America, to the West Indies and to the Baltic. There was also an extensive coasting trade, some of it very local. The schooner drying her sails while a boy skylarks in the mud is the *Colleen* built at Barnstaple in 1880. The iron or steel barque on the right-hand side of the picture has probably come for repairs in the excellent local shipbuilding yard, in Edwardian times run by Robert Cock & Sons. The stone tower was built by Thomas B. Chanter, a leading local shipowner, for use as a watchtower so that gangs could be ready to discharge local traders as soon as they berthed in the harbour. Much of this hard work was done by women stevedores in mid-Victorian times

83 *Below* Ilfracombe, now only a seaside resort, in Victorian times was a thriving harbour with local shipbuilding and trade to the continent and to North America. The vessel on board which this photograph was taken, probably in the 1870s, while she was lying at Ilfracombe Harbour was a brigantine. Some details are obscure, but she could be one of the polacca brigantines which were unique to the Bristol Channel in Victorian times and probably copied from the Swedish vessels which frequently discharged timber in Bideford and other Bristol Channel ports in the early nineteenth century

84 *Right* This picture tells much of the reality of a rural seaport in late Victorian times. It shows Irsha, the west part of Appledore. Note the roofs of the houses. The people in them lived hard, worked hard and drank hard and often lived upstairs and paid no rent. The boat on davits belonged to the chief local pilot, known as 'Long Haired Jan', and it was ready to be lowered in a hurry should a vessel require a pilot when the tide came in. West Appledore in particular had a bad reputation for fighting and for hostility to strangers. Certainly the girls don't seem to be giving these painters of the 1890s much elbow room. Only one of the five has shoes and stockings and one of them seems to be losing her knickers, though such was the standard of living that she was lucky to have any. The post and heavy chain were used for mooring vessels on the beach

85 *Left* The quayside at Bideford, in late Victorian times. The old, hogged, brig *Arendal* is, as her name suggests, from Norway. The big three-masted *slättoppare* is probably Russian/Finnish. The ketch nearest the camera is local. This magnificent photograph gives some impression of what Bideford and many other small ports looked like at the height of their prosperity in Victorian times

86 Clovelly, the famous North Devon beauty spot, had a granite-walled harbour used by local fishing and trading vessels, but it was far too small for the visiting paddle steamers with their hoards of tourists. So these people were landed in over-loaded local fishing boats and they scrambled up the pebble beach to spend their money to the benefit of the poor local inhabitants, who lived every bit as rough as the people of West Appledore. The steamer is the *Westward Ho!* and the photograph was taken before she was rebuilt in 1912

87 *Right above* Padstow in north Cornwall at the outer limits of the Bristol Channel, if you accept that it goes so far, was a shipbuilding centre and the home of a big fleet of merchant vessels; again, it was a community which had as its industry the carrying trade. In mid-Victorian times Padstow was a place of emigration to Canada. We choose this particular photograph because it shows so well the old-time burdensome full-bowed schooner next to the quay and in the middle of the photograph a big decked Severn trow, one of the sailing barges of the Bristol Channel. She was the *Theodore*, built at Saul on the Sharpness Canal in 1871

88 The granite walled harbour at Newquay in Cornwall looks old but in fact is another product of the nineteenth century. It was built to facilitate the export of the products of local mines and the import of coal and so prospered that in 1879 164 vessels used the harbour. Agricultural products and many other cargoes also passed in and out.

Here local vessels are seen lying at the quays, the *Belle of the Plym*, the *William Henry*, the *Agnes Louisa*, the *Fairy Maid* and the *Fairy Belle*, just a few of the nearly 200 smacks, ketches, schooners and brigantines owned in Newquay between 1818 and 1916

89 The entrance to Barry Dock in South Wales in Edwardian times. The vessels nearest the camera are Bristol Channel pilot cutters (see Plate 74). Those to the south near the crane on the breakwater are Bristol Channel trading ketches, like the *Wave* in Plate 76 and the *Lily* and the *Three Sisters* in Plate 81. All are taking advantage of free facilities to shelter given by the Barry Dock authorities to vessels of these classes

90 *Right* At the end of the Edwardian era the steel barque *Glimpt* lies in Newport Docks waiting to load. Newport Docks were a product of the coal age – their chief function the export of the products of the local pits. The old Town Dock was opened in 1842 and extended in 1854. The Alexandra North Dock was opened in 1875 and named after the wife of the future King Edward VII

Wales

THE GREAT ports of South Wales – Newport, Cardiff, Barry, Swansea – were all in their modern form products of the Victorian era. The rise of a worldwide demand for coal which came with the worldwide use of steam power in the second half of the nineteenth century meant the development of these ports to serve the great coal fields of South Wales and other local industries as they developed. One of the big factors in the rise of the Welsh ports was the development of the steamship which required that coal should be deposited all over the world to be used as bunkers by vessels on long voyages.

Other Welsh ports, all the way around the coast, served fishing fleets, the packet service to Ireland and the great trade overseas and around the coasts which was carried on in Victorian and Edwardian times in locally-owned wooden sailing vessels. North Wales has been fortunate in the excellent maritime recording and publishing which has been done in recent years by Aled Eames of the University of Wales and by the County Archives of Gwynedd.

452.

91 *Left* Coal is poured into the empty steel hull of the barque *Lady Isabella* at Cardiff while some of her crew gossip with the crew of the tramp steamer *Harrington* of West Hartlepool (built at Port Glasgow in 1872), which is waiting to load in the berth. Cardiff was another product of the Victorian age and of the age of coal. Its modern history began with the completion of what was later known as the Bute West Dock in 1839. Rapid development in the next 60 years made Cardiff one of the major ports in the country

92 *Above* Barry was the last of the great South Wales coal ports to be developed. It was a product of late Victorian times and this photograph shows Barry Dock filled with steamers and big steel sailing vessels in the 1890s. Most of them, like the typical late Victorian tramp steamer *Margaret Jones*, built at South Shields in 1889 and owned in Cardiff, in the foreground, have come to load coal

93 This photograph, and the next one, have appeared in more than one book in the past, but they are so remarkable that their reproduction again is fully justified. This one shows Swansea in the 1840s before the floating docks were built, filled with the flat-bottomed wooden sailing ships which were the ordinary merchant vessels of the period, and with a few paddle steamers. The vessel sitting upright on the mud in the centre of the picture is the *Countess of Bective* built in 1843. The vessel against the dock wall just beyond her is the *Mary Dugdale*, built at Hull in 1835

94 *Above right* And from the same set of photographs in the National Maritime Museum taken in Swansea in the 1840s by the Revd Calvert Jones is this one showing eight square-rigged ships, a smack, a schooner, and two paddle tugs with funnels like those of Stephenson's *Rocket*.
This photograph may, incidentally, antedate Fox Talbot's famous photograph of the newly launched steamship *Great Britain* and thus be the first photograph showing steamships ever taken

95 *Right* Forty years later, in May 1888, the locally-owned wooden barque *Epsilon* built by George Cox at Cleave Houses, Bideford, lay in Swansea Docks, now enormously developed, discharging her cargo of ore from South America through a wooden shute into a barge with a crew of one. This copper ore trade from the west coast of South America to Swansea was one of the most exacting for wooden ships and their crews, including rounding Cape Horn twice on each voyage, once with a very difficult cargo. George Cox built more than a dozen of these barques for the trade between 1858 and 1866

96 At the mouth of Tenby Harbour three sailing trawlers from Brixham in Devon are seen lying aground at low tide. The big beam trawl is clearly visible hanging on the port side of the trawler in the middle of the picture. Large numbers of Brixham trawlers used Tenby as a fishing base and some Brixham men married locally and settled in the Welsh port

97 *Above right* Porthmadog in Gwynedd was a creation of Victorian industrial enterprise and expansion, a text book case of a small community building an artificial harbour to export a local product – slate – which became a centre of shipbuilding and shipowning with trade over half the earth. Here is the harbour, first opened in 1824, as it was in 1877, literally packed with shipping

98 Porthmadog was famous as a shipbuilding place. In its yards the small wooden merchant sailing ship was developed to a very high degree of efficiency in the last decade of Queen Victoria's reign. This photograph shows the three-masted schooner *Isallt II*, 'in frame'. To build a wooden ship of this quality and size now would cost a large fortune

99   One of the finest products of Porthmadog shipyards
was the three-masted schooner *Frau Minna Petersen,*
here shown at anchor. Her trans-Atlantic voyages in the
1920s made her one of the last merchant sailing vessels to
trade on deep water from a home port in Britain

100 This is another example of a shipping place where there was no port or harbour in the legal or conventional sense. It was the practice at Penmaenmawr to load slate from quarries in the mountains into coastal vessels lying at a jetty just off the beach. The business depended on local knowledge of the weather, vigilance and skilled seamanship. In fact, it was so risky that people took such care and developed such expertise that relatively few vessels were lost in this kind of commercial operation round the coasts of Britain

101   Langton Dock, Liverpool, one sunny afternoon in the early 1890s. The steamships are still all heavily rigged with square sails; the era of the twin-screw steamer and the thoroughly reliable engine had only just dawned. The schooner at the quay at the right-hand side of the picture is the *Lord Mostyn* of Beaumaris built at Rhuddlan in 1844 and owned in Amlwch

102   *Right* This vessel, the wooden barque *Ebenezer* built in 1869, has not been wrecked. She has simply been rigged down by her own crew in anticipation of a passage through the Manchester Ship Canal. A rigging job of this kind was well within the powers of the crew of an ordinary wooden merchant ship, and indeed the *Ebenezer* was built only a generation after it was the custom to dismantle the upper rigging of such ships in bad weather at sea. Skills like these are now among the most completely lost of all forms of high craftsmanship

Liverpool and the North West

For the period covered by this book Liverpool was the second port in the kingdom. By 1820 it was connected by a canal with the textile towns of Lancashire and Yorkshire, with the developing industrial midlands and the potteries of Staffordshire. For most of Queen Victoria's reign it was the principal terminus in Britain for the North Atlantic passenger trade, first in sail and then in steam. But the smaller ports of the north west prospered as well in the nineteenth century and their harbours were developed and dock facilities improved. Maryport, White-haven, Workington, Millom, shipped huge quantities of coal or iron ore. Whitehaven had a trade with North America and an important shipyard. Millom was a centre of small shipbuilding, as was also Glasson Dock. Fleetwood, a nineteenth-century creation, was an important fishing port. Fleets of fishing vessels and many small merchant sailing vessels sailed from the Isle of Man and there is still a big iron square-rigged sailing ship afloat, the *Star of India*, kept as a Museum ship at San Diego, California, which was built at Ramsey in 1863.

103 and **104** This photograph and that which follows
are among the earliest known photographs showing a
port. They were taken in Dublin (it is not certain that
no. 103 is Dublin) by Fox Talbot in the early 1840s,
somewhat before the photographs of Swansea in Plates 93
and 94. They show just what would be expected, large
numbers of small, full-bodied, wooden merchant sailing
ships with the complex rigging imposed by the use of
natural fibre rope – no iron wire – and very simple port
facilities, if any at all, on the quays for loading and
discharging cargo

NDING STAGE. LIVERPOOL.   PWS 1109.

105 *Left* Liverpool was involved in many trades, and on a huge scale by the standards of Victorian and Edwardian times, but it is for the trans-Atlantic passenger trade that the period is most remembered. Here the white Star Line's first *Adriatic*, built in 1872 and the holder in that year of a new record for the westward passage, is lying in the Mersey. She was broken up in 1889

106 *Left below* The crowded landing stage at Liverpool with paddle steamer ferries, the one nearest the camera loading for New Brighton, and the White Star liner *Germanic*, built in 1875 and not scrapped until 1950, at anchor in the background. The steam ferry services were an important factor in Liverpool's development. In late Victorian times they carried millions of people every year

107 *Below* Against the Liverpool water front the White Star liner *Teutonic* lies at anchor. She was built in 1889

108 *Left* The White Star Line's tender *Magnetic* lying off the landing stage at Liverpool. Two Mersey ferries may be seen at the stage itself. The largest liners such as the *Teutonic* were obliged to lie at anchor in the Mersey and embark passengers and luggage by tenders such as this. The *Magnetic* was built by Harland & Wolff at Belfast in 1891

110 *Below* Sailing vessels running up the Mersey on the flood tide were so common as to be part of the daily scene. John Masefield has a splendid description of them in his book *New Chum*. This vessel against a background of docks and landing stages, is the brigantine *Brothers*, built in Prince Edward Island, Canada, in 1860, and she is racing up to catch the tide to enter Garston

109 *Left below* Looking somewhat seaworn, the steel four-masted barque *Wanderer* lies in the Mersey. The subject of a poem by John Masefield, this extremely handsome vessel was unlucky from her launch in 1890 to her loss in collision with a German steamer in 1907. Many members of her crews were killed in accidents and she was more than once involved in 'casualties', mishaps of various kinds

111 *Left* This delightful picture shows the bows of the barque *Anne Gambles* built at Whitehaven in 1860 just after she had been completed. Standing immediately in front of the figurehead is its original, the wife of Captain John Gambles, who stands with her. As far as we know this delightful harbour scene is unique in its juxtaposition of vessel, master, figurehead, and model

112 *Below* Port St Mary, Isle of Man, with the schooner *Margaret Garton*, built there in 1877. The photograph is of especial interest because it is the only known picture of a heavily-rigged British schooner with square topsail and flying topgallant, but with a running bowsprit. The vessel was later converted to normal rig with a fixed peg bowsprit

113 *Above* The magnificent four-masted barque *Lynton*
is towed to sea from Maryport by a local twin-funnelled
tug. The *Lynton* was built in 1894 on the Mersey and is a
splendid example of a late Victorian big merchant sailing
ship. She was torpedoed in 1917 when registered at the
island of Vårdö in the Åland Islands in the Finnish
archipelago and owned by Robert Mattsson of Mariehamn

114   The trade of the Clyde with its island settlements and relatively sheltered water provided employment for a number of trading smacks – single-masted sailing vessels – well into the present century. Loch Ranza was one of these little island harbours with a strong local trade and a fishing industry. Here fishermen are seen coming ashore from their boats (the date is 8 August 1903) while three trading smacks, the nearest the *Katharine McMillan* built at Ardrossan in 1861 and owned in Rothesay, can be seen in the background

115   *Right* The true vessel of the west coast of Scotland was, however, the steam puffer. These were small steam cargo vessels built to dimensions to enable them to pass through the Forth and Clyde Canal – or to go some of the way through to canal-side wharves – and yet able to trade to the small communities in the Western Isles. They even had upright boilers to save length, clearly seen in this photograph of the *Tom Moore* loading from carts at a wharf somewhere at the Glasgow end of the canal

Scotland

THE PORTS and harbours of Scotland are associated in most people's minds with the great shipbuilders of the Clyde, Aberdeen and Dundee. The industry on the Clyde underwent phenomenal development in Victorian times and produced some of the finest ships, both sail and steam, the world has ever seen. But besides these great centres there were many smaller harbours and shipping places where trade was carried on and which were the home ports of great fishing fleets employing very distinctive types of sailing fishing vessels. The many island communities were entirely dependent upon communication by sea, and their harbours often tended to become the centres of local life.

116 *Left* The ports of the Clyde in the 70 years before the First World War are associated with a great outburst of shipbuilding and shipowning activity, reaching its climax towards the end of the century. Lying in her home port the *Loch Tay*, an iron full-rigged ship built in Glasgow in 1869 for the Australian trade, illustrates a most successful era in Glasgow's history

117 *Right* Scots fishermen lived simply. This row of cottages was photographed at Ballantrae in August 1909

118 *Below* Of a later era is the steel full-rigged ship *Talus*, built in 1891 on the Clyde and here photographed in Greenock. With her midship's house extended to the full width of the vessel she was a fine example of the last square-rigged merchant sailing ships. At the time this photograph was taken she was owned in Greenock and was employed principally in trade to the west coast of South America from the Bristol Channel

119 *Left above* This is another side of Aberdeen maritime activity, the iron four-masted barque *Port Jackson*, built at Aberdeen by Alexander Hall & Co in 1882, and described as one of the most beautiful iron vessels ever launched. She spent most of her life in trade to and from Australia, latterly with cadets as a merchant training ship. The training she gave was a thorough professional preparation for potential merchant ship mates rather than the brief adventure training given in many of the 'tall ships' today. The photograph, showing various shore people on the poop and elsewhere, was probably taken soon after her completion

121 *Above* The characteristics of Scottish fishing sailing vessels in Victorian times are clearly illustrated in this photograph of the harbour at Stornoway in the Hebrides taken in 1908. They are dipping luggers, double-ended, with little overhanging gear, ideal for packing tight in the small harbours of both coasts of Scotland, yet very seaworthy

120 *Left* Aberdeen was a centre of shipbuilding in the Victorian era, a great fishing port and the home port of merchant vessels trading all over the world. This photograph shows some of the large fishing fleet, and in the foreground women coming ashore from a ferry which was pulled across the harbour by winding a fixed wire cable on a drum mounted in the boat. The handle of this gear and the fly wheel are clearly visible

122 *Left* Dundee was one of the principal ports of the British arctic whaling industry, using wooden steam vessels heavily rigged as barques or barquentines. But it was also, of course, a shipbuilding centre and the centre of import of the raw material for the great jute spinning and weaving industry, dependent, in late Victorian times, on cargoes of baled jute brought from Calcutta and Chittagong in steel sailing ships. Here is the magnificent four-masted barque *Saragossa*, built at Dundee in 1902, discharging jute in the docks

123 *Below* This detailed picture shows the north part of Stonehaven harbour with the barrels for packing salted fish, the nets and baskets for carrying fish from the boats

124 *Above* South of Aberdeen is Stonehaven, a fishing and coasting harbour, here seen in Edwardian times with its fleet of lug-rigged fishing vessels, characteristic of this part of Scotland

125 *Below* South of St Andrew's is Crail, Fife. In the photograph a fisherman wearing the old leather sea boots which were all that was available before the mass production of rubber boots, is putting lobster pots ashore on a slipway in the quiet little harbour